Fu  l

Search Press
London & New York

Introduction

To make foil models all you need is a roll of foil. The fewer odd pieces of foil you use, the more stable your model will be. But if you do want to fix one piece of foil on another — for instance, a hat on a human figure — you need pins, a suitable adhesive (ask your supplier), and scissors to trim things from time to time.

The best foil for silver foil sculpture is that sold in rolls as 'cooking foil' with a silver metallic coating on both sides.

You can mould a flat sheet of foil into almost as many shapes as a piece of clay. The foil is cheap, non-toxic and has an attractive glistening appearance. Coloured foils are obtainable and as a variation the foil can be dipped into emulsion or gloss paint.

Before you try to make a model get used to the feel of the material. Tear off a sheet and try rolling it into a ball. Then press the ball into various solid shapes: cubes, pyramids, and so on. Roll some foil into a long stick and bend it at one end to make a handle. Twist it into a snake and try bending it round and joining the ends together to make a ring or a hoop. Tear off another rectangular strip of foil. Fold it down the middle and press the ends firmly together to make a boat.

Basic shapes

Human figure

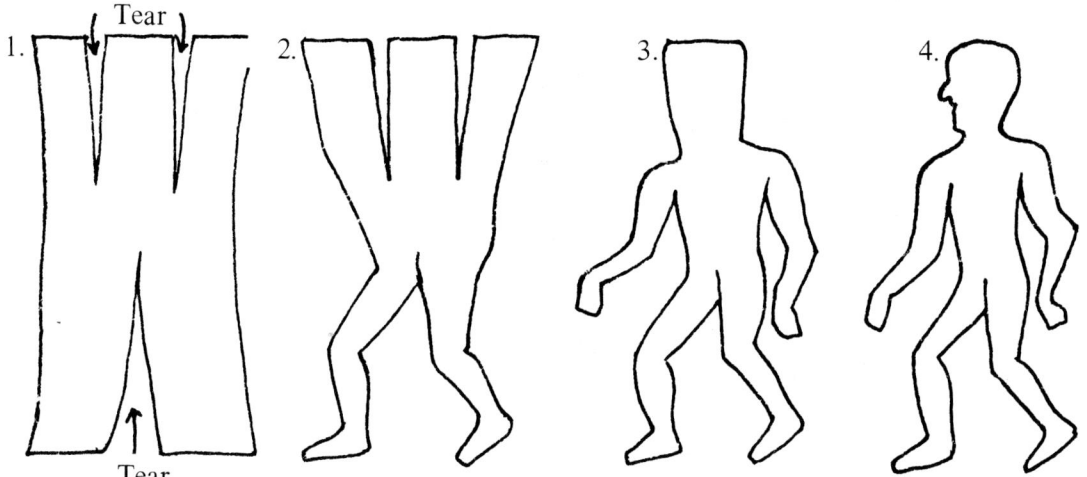

1. Tear / Tear
2.
3.
4.

Horse

1. Tear / Tear
2.
3.
4.

3

Old man
with stick

The method you use for your first figure can be used for all kinds of foil people. To model the old man with a stick cut out a rectangle of foil. Make two tears at one end and one tear in the middle of the other end. The three sections at one end are to be modelled as arms and a head, and the two sections at the other end as legs. Because the old man is long and spindly you need a long piece of silver paper and you have to make long tears. When you have made the general shape of legs, arms and body, press out the shape of neck, head and other details. Use a circular piece of foil for the hat and roll a long strip of foil into a twisty walking stick. Wrap one of the man's hands round the stick and press so that it is held firmly. Fix the hat with a strong adhesive or a pin.

Dog and rooster

This lively dual animal scene might be an illustration to one of Aesop's or La Fontaine's fables and can stand as an example of the various group scenes that are possible with silver foil. You can work indefinitely through legends, fairy tales and so on, although animal stories will provide the easiest and most popular subjects. The column for the rooster is made from a rectangle of foil as long as you wish. The rooster itself is made following the basic instructions for birds and the crow (pages 26 and 27), but adjusting the projections for comb and wings appropriately. Stick the bird to the column with a dab of adhesive. Mould a basic animal or horse shape and adjust it for the dog, but make sure that the balance is right. Give the column an inserted coin for stability or a thick base.

Skier

When you have made a satisfactory human figure model, bend the knees to give an impression of speed. Make the hat and any extra pieces of clothing separately and stick them into place. Use four long strips for the skis and ski sticks. Put the skier on the skis, fold a strip of foil round each foot and press very hard so that the feet are held firm and the skier can stand up. Fold the hands round the ski sticks and again pinch hard so that the sticks are firm. Experiment with the skier's position until he seems to be speeding over the snow.

Race-horse and jockey

The foil race-horse must be slim but strong enough to take a foil jockey. Model the horse from a rectangle of foil. Experiment with its position so that it stands up yet gives an impression of speed. When making the jockey add extra foil to the legs to make breeches and boots. To give the effect of racing colours use coloured foil or gloss paint.

Clowns

Clowns with baggy clothes, funny hats and big feet lend themselves to foil modelling. You will probably need to add extra foil to the body and legs to give a baggy clothing effect. You need extra foil to make the over-sized shoes which are pressed over the feet. Flatten the soles of the shoes against a hard surface until the clown stays erect. Make a cone of foil and twist the top to form a pointed hat. Try folding a strip of foil to make a ruff, but if you are unsuccessful use scissors to get the shape you need. A thin piece of foil rolled out and bent to form a circle will make a hoop for the clown to hold and keep him from falling over.

Bull

This stubborn and fierce creature should be made with all the tenacity and liveliness of the creature in the ring. Start with a basic animal shape but make sure to provide additional tabs for the horns and more foil for the powerful flanks and body. Make sure that you establish the right tension between legs and bowed head.

Ship

Use a large rectangle of foil for the hull. Fold the foil lengthways and press the ends together. Then make a box shape for the cabins that fits into the centre of the ship, and stick it in position. Roll strips of foil into funnel shapes and stick them on the cabin.

Crinoline lady

To make a crinoline lady use a rectangle of foil as long as the depth of the dress. Provide pleats and pinch carefully into the shape of the waist. Make the top half of the figure and match up with the skirt to check that they are in proportion. Make a bodice from a strip of foil with a tear in the middle of one end. Place the two sections over the shoulders of the figure, wrap them round the body, and keep in place with a dab of adhesive. Experiment with a crumpled piece of foil until you get the right bonnet shape and stick it on the figure's head.

Horse and tree

Make the horse as for the horse shape (page 3), but ensure that its rear legs are integrated with the tree, either by twisting and gluing or by the slightly more difficult means of cutting a large enough piece to produce both tree and horse. The rectangle used for the tree should be as long as you wish but always in proportion to the horse. Similar combinations of flora and fauna are possible.

Boxers

Make two basic foil human figures but leave the ends of the arms as handless points. Make the boxing gloves separately: press the gloves over the end of the arms and pinch hard; a little adhesive will make sure they do not fall off. Add foil shorts and boots. These extra items can be in different coloured foils; otherwise use gloss paint.

Vikings

Vikings are good action figures. Study pictures of Viking shields, helmets, swords and faces. Then model them with foil. Make a cup-shaped helmet, cut out wings and stick one on either side of the helmet. Stick the helmet on the Viking's head.

Viking ship _(overleaf)_

This impressive vessel calls for two sheets of foil, one red and one silver. The pennant, sail stripes and shields are made individually and glued separately to the appropriate parts. The ship itself is made from a long wide rectangle of silver foil. Make it as elegant as possible but remember that it must have a fairly wide, flat base to stand on. The mast is a rolled and twisted length of foil passed through two slits in the sail to stand on a flat solid base glued with a dab of adhesive to the inside of the ship.

Giraffes *(on previous page)*

Start your giraffe with a long rectangular sheet of silver foil. Make two long tears at each end to allow for the long neck and legs. Then press and roll out the neck, legs, body and tail. Make the head from another piece of foil and have enough foil protruding to shape the horns and ears. Press out the shape of the mouth with the blade of a knife or scissors. Then press the head into position on the top of the neck. Bend the legs so that the giraffe is balanced and can stand up. Finish off with yellow and black gloss paint if you wish.

Cowboy

To make a cowboy on a horse you need two rectangular sheets of foil, one larger than the other. The larger sheet is for the horse. Make two tears at each end of this piece. At one end the three sections are to be made into two front legs and a head. At the other end model the three sections as two hind legs and a tail. Make the body last. If the head proves difficult make it separately and press it onto the neck, with adhesive if necessary. Then make a saddle, and pin or stick it on the horse's body. Model a human figure with the smaller piece of foil and match up with the horse for size. The effect of chaps can be obtained by squeezing the foil along the backs of the cowboy's legs. Use small sheets of foil to make a hat, belt, stirrups and spurs. Put the cowboy on the saddle and keep him in place with a pin. Change his position from time to time.

St. George and the dragon

The knight is a foil figure decorated with a helmet and shield and carrying a lance. You can stick on stirrups and helmet plumes. For the dragon use a large sheet of foil and model one leg at a time, pinching out claws at the end of the feet. As the head is large it will be necessary to make it separately and then either stick or press it firmly onto the dragon's long silver neck. You can stick on large bulging lumps of foil as eyes and extra pieces of foil as wings.

Reindeer

This superbly proud animal needs a piece of foil big enough to provide pieces for the antlers at one end and the solid base at the other. Follow the basic animal shape and make sure that the antlers are approximately one third of the height of the entire piece. Aim for a combination of elegance and power.

Elephant

Practise modelling the elephant's head with its large ears, trunk and tusks. You need a large sheet of foil for the body and legs. If you have some used pieces of foil which are no good for further modelling, put them into the elephant's body, otherwise he may look flat and thin. When you have made the body and four legs attach the head and trunk.

Eagle descending on prey

For this piece you can either try to make all the parts in one continuous line from one large piece of foil, or combine separate pieces, gluing and twisting them as seems appropriate. The bird can be as eagle-like as you wish, and follows the essential bird pattern (page 26); remember to accommodate the wing span if you follow this model carefully. It is better if the bird appears to curve 'naturally' out of the tree, but not essential. The fleeing rabbit below takes only a few minutes.

Birds

Silver foil birds need care since you must add wings, beak and unusual legs. It is better to practise making these items individually before trying to complete the model. Start with a sheet of foil; make two tears at one end and one tear at the other end. Model the three sections into a neck and wings. You will need to pad out the body with extra foil, pressing it firmly to hold it in position. Roll out the two sections to make long legs and bend them in the middle. Make the head and long bill and stick this piece on the neck. Finally make the feet and fix them to the legs. Bend the legs and feet so that the foil stork is well balanced and stands up.

Crow

To make a crow or a similar bird pad out the body with foil. Then decide where the head, wings and legs are to go. Make these items separately. Pull out two pieces of foil from the body, one on either side, wrap the ends of the wings round them and pinch hard. Turn back the wings and if necessary use scissors for the required shape. Attach the head and legs to the body. Make the clawed feet and fix them to the legs. You may need a spot of strong adhesive to keep everything in place.

Father Christmas

The silver gleam of foil lends itself to Christmas decorations. Make a foil figure with boots and a long beard as the basis of a Father Christmas. Dress him with a red foil coat. Cut two long strips for the sledge runners and fold these to give strength. Cut a number of foil slats and fold them round the runners to make a firm join by pressing hard. A foil sack is easily made and placed on the sledge. You can fill the sack with colourfully wrapped sweets or chocolates. Model the reindeer as for a horse but give it slender legs and a small tail. Leave two pieces of foil protruding on either side of the head. Make the antlers and then twist and press the foil round them until they are firm. The other two pieces of foil will form ears and can be finished off with scissors.

Flowers

To make flowers, roll out small pieces of foil for stamens. Pleat a strip of foil into a trumpet shape and wrap it round the stamens. Use four squares of foil for petals. Hold square, fold to opposite corners and press firmly, bending the top back. Then make a stem, leaving some foil at the base of the petals; squeeze it until the petals are held tightly.

Water Lily

Cut out four water lily leaf shapes as a basis for the flower.
Make four small petals and stamens. Wrap petals round
stamens and press to hold. Add larger petals until you
have a flower of the required size. Add spots of strong
adhesive to make sure that the petals do not slip apart.

Acknowledgments

Text and models by Isobel and John Milsome
Photographs by John Morfett

First published in Great Britain in 1978 by Search Press
Limited, 2-10 Jerdan,Place, London SW6 5PT

If readers in Britain and Ireland cannot buy the materials
listed or mentioned, they should write to Search Press
Limited, 2-10 Jerdan Place, London SW6 5PT.

Made and printed in Spain by Editorial Elexpuru Hnos,
SA Zamudio-Bilbao

ISBN 0 85532 492 9